Praise for *Design Your Day*

I love the message of this book: get more done by doing less. Often, we think that productivity is the result of doing more, but rarely does it turn out that way. If you struggle, like I do, to focus on what matters most, then *Design Your Day* will be a breath of fresh air. Read it, then live it.

—JEFF GOINS, bestselling author of *The Art of Work*

Who doesn't need more hours in their day? With so many responsibilities to juggle and hats to wear, it can feel like the days fly by and your to-do list flies out the window. By the end of the day you wonder to yourself, "what did I even do?" and "why didn't the things I needed to accomplish actually get done?" If you can identify with this, you don't want to miss this book. I can't think of anyone better to teach you to make the most of your life than Claire.

—ALLISON VESTERFELT, author of *Packing Light: Thoughts on Living Life with Less Baggage*

I'm making more than a few changes based on the super-practical concepts in this book. Claire does an amazing job of clearing the air and helping you make the most important things the most important things. I've always been a goal-oriented person but this book is helping me take it to another level!

—JOËL MALM, founder of Su and author of *Vision Map*

D0150334

There are plenty of do-more-in-less-time strategies out there. Claire isn't about doing that with shortcuts. Rather, she's all about identifying the right goals, and acting with purpose so that you really can do more in less time, while still achieving the things you value. With clarity and insight, her methods are an antidote to idle busyness.

—JUSTIN WISE, founder and CEO of Think Digital

Goals are everything when it comes to business and life in general. Claire couldn't have done a better job defining how to set purposeful goals for yourself. There are a lot of books out there about goal setting. This one is special. Meaningful goals matter, and *Design Your Day* helps you understand how to give your goals purpose, and more importantly, how to achieve them using a simple and effective strategy. Bravo Claire!

—SCOTT WARNER, CEO, Gigg

Productivity isn't just about the grind; it's about the decisions you make about how you work. Work hard to work well. *Design Your Day* will show you how.

—ALLI WORTHINGTON, COO, Propel Women and author of *Breaking Busy*

DESIGN YOUR DAY

DESIGN YOUR DAY

be more productive,
set better goals,
and live life on purpose

CLAIRE DIAZ-ORTIZ

MOODY PUBLISHERS

CHICAGO

© 2016 by
CLAIRE DIAZ-ORTIZ

Edited by Pam Pugh
Interior design: Ragont Design and Erik M. Peterson
Cover design: Erik M. Peterson
Author photo: Jose Diaz-Ortiz

Library of Congress Cataloging-in-Publication Data

Diaz-Ortiz, Claire, 1982- author.
 Design your day : be more productive, set better goals, and live life on purpose
/ Claire Diaz-Ortiz.
   pages cm
 Includes bibliographical references.
 ISBN 978-0-8024-1294-2
 1. Time management. 2. Goal (Psychology) I. Title.
 BF637.T5D53 2015
 650.1--dc23
            2015030185

All websites and phone numbers listed herein are accurate at the time of publication but may change in the future or cease to exist. The listing of website references and resources does not imply publisher endorsement of the site's entire contents. Groups and organizations are listed for informational purposes, and listing does not imply publisher endorsement of their activities.

We hope you enjoy this book from Moody Publishers. Our goal is to provide high-quality, thought-provoking books and products that connect truth to your real needs and challenges. For more information on other books and products written and produced from a biblical perspective, go to www.moodypublishers. com or write to:

Moody Publishers
820 N. LaSalle Boulevard
Chicago, IL 60610

1 3 5 7 9 10 8 6 4 2

Printed in the United States of America

CONTENTS

GETTING STARTED: BIG ROCKS

It is 5:00 p.m. and you're late to pick up a small, uniformed child at soccer practice. Although the day is mostly over, you feel like it never really began. You vaguely remember an alarm going off in a darkened morning, and a rushed hour of kids and notebooks and cereal flying. A big yellow bus passed in and out of your vision. Then a series of errands and meetings and phone calls paraded by for hours on end—a squashed sandwich in a plastic bag providing you a few minutes of quiet calm.

Throughout it all, there was the coffee. *May I never have to live a day without coffee*, you muse. A to-do list, sitting next to you on the passenger seat in your car, has twenty-seven items on it, only two of which you managed to cross off today. You didn't even really get started.

"But today was an unusual day," you rationalize. "So many unexpected things came up."

"Tomorrow will be better," you promise yourself, only slightly wincing.

It's not a lie if you believe it, right?

When it comes to living the life we want to live, there are good days and there are bad days. We all have bad days. Days where the car breaks down when you're in labor, the puppy eats your college thesis, and the basement floods the Christmas presents away. And sometimes we can't change these days. But there are many days—like when life zips by in a series of flashes and suddenly you're on the way to pick up that child from practice and your to-do list didn't get any shorter—that we can do something about. And learning to change these days is one of the most important lessons we will ever learn. Your particular day might differ—replace the kids and breakfast cereal with lattes and late-night graduate school study groups—but the idea is the same. Whatever it is that matters most to you in life—your family, your health, your faith, your friends—will suffer if you don't learn to live your days well.

Many of us have seen the experiment with the rocks and the jar. If you are new to this idea, go get a few big rocks, a ton of small pebbles, and a large glass jar. You'll find that if you put the pebbles in the jar first and then try to put in the big rocks, you'll have trouble fitting everything in. Do things the other way around, though, and you're golden. Put your big rocks in the jar fist, and then fill the jar's air pockets up with pebbles. Ta-da! It fits.

Life is the same way. It's easy to fill up a day or a life with an endless series of pebbles and then not have the time, energy, or resources to fit in the big rocks. A life well designed is about making sure that the important stuff stays important, day in and day out.

Days shouldn't live themselves, and this is a book about making sure they don't.

This book takes part in two acts.

Together, they walk you through the Do Less method, a productivity and goal-setting model I designed to help folks get more done in less time and succeed more often. Close readers will notice that "DO" is not just one of the most used words in the English language, but is also (fantastically, I might add) a word made up of the initials of my last name.

The **Do Less** method is about taking back your time, and giving it to someone who really knows what they're doing.

You!

In Part One, we'll look at the first step, **Decide**. This is where you'll think hard about what is important and what is not in the year or season you have ahead. This is where you

Summer

pare down on the nonessentials and learn to clarify what you really want. Remember that what you want is all about what you value in this world.

In Part Two, we'll dive into Organize. We'll put key productivity strategies in place to reach the smart goals you've set for yourself, day by day, year by year. Specifically, **Organize** follows through four steps: Limit, Edit, Streamline, and Stop (**LESS**).

The Do Less method will help you win more often and love your life better along the way.

PART ONE: DECIDE

"If you don't know where you are going,
you'll end up someplace else."
—Yogi Berra

First, we're going to decide what matters. Then, we'll figure out how to get you where you're going.

The first step in getting where you're going is deciding what you want, and thus the Do Less Method starts with a big D.

Decide.

It's time to think long and hard about what you want. We'll start by setting an overarching theme for the year or season ahead, and then we'll jump down into creating powful goals for your life and work.

WORD OF
THE YEAR

For the last few years, I've done something smart. Now, I'm not always doing smart things, so believe me when I say that this is something to write home about. What have I done? I've chosen a word of the year.

I got the idea from a book, and it's worked well to bring my life a greater sense of direction and fulfillment. I'm now such a fan that I'll shout it from my handy nearby mountaintop:

> Each year, you should choose a word to
> represent the year you have in front of you.

Think long and hard about one word that will serve as a guidepost for what you want to do and be in the year to come. And remember that a year needn't start January 1

—you can start your year at any time! One word that will remind you of what's important when you need it most. One word to mean everything you want your year to be, and one word that will be a guiding light when times get tough and you're not clear on what your priorities are..

There aren't a lot of rules. Your word can be a verb or a noun. It can be long. It can be short. A word that has funny sounds in it or a word that rolls off the tongue. Depending on the type of year you're going for, some examples of great words might be: Breathe, Push, Persevere, Give, Abundance, Direction, Moxie, Contentment.

The first year I did this exercise, I needed it badly. I was in a season of overwhelm, and so choosing my word—REST—felt like taking a big old breath of fresh air. Those four letters meant the world to me.

It wasn't all smooth sailing, though, and I made a lot of mistakes during the year. By publicly stating my word, I also provoked some interesting responses in others. Many folks who read about my word of the year talked about it when they saw me—or, even better, mentioned it when they were asking me to do something! A number of times I received a note or call along the lines of, "I know you said your word of the year was REST, but I was wondering if you could . . ."

This alone let me know that something about publicly stating my word of the year was working. And not just for me to know my own priorities, but for others to know them as well. (Yes, they may still have been asking me to do something, but they were at least conscious that I was likely to say it wasn't the right year for me to agree!)

The next year, with great deliberation, I chose a new word: RENEW. After a year of rest, I was ready for balance, and looked for a guidepost to help me carefully choose what I would take on in my personal and professional life in this time of measured growth. I wasn't resting, but I wasn't going hog wild either.

This past year, I mixed it up, going digital with my word of the year and choosing not a word, but a hashtag.

#BanBusy

As a digital gal, living in a digital world, the act of choosing a hashtag seemed more me than ever before. The point's the same, after all. It is one short, powerful idea promising to revolutionize the way I think about what I do. And so #banbusy aimed to help me be mindful of one of the scarcest resources I have: time.

#banbusy was my aim to help myself. And, as in past years, it did just that. On really bad days, I'd wear the #banbusy necklace someone sent me to remind me of just what I had signed up to. And, day-by-day, I worked hard to be a steward of my time, and a minder of not making my life *too* full.

The first step in deciding what you want to achieve or how you want to feel is about framing all those larger decisions as part of a larger theme. This theme is your word of the year (or your word for a season).

Think hard about a word that will help guide you in your upcoming season of life. Find a powerful word that encompasses the things you want to accomplish, yes, but the way you want to feel as well.

Don't jump into things. Try one word on for size. Then try another.

Give yourself time to find the right word (or, yes, hashtag) to express what you want the year ahead of you to be.

This process may take days or it may take weeks. You may start with one word, try it on for size, and discard it for another. That's fine. That's good, in fact! More than anything, you need to find a word that feels right, sounds right, and means right.

Find the **word of the year** that's **the word of you.**

serendipitous - making fortunate discoveries by accident

HOW TO SET
SMART GOALS

IDEATE

O nce you have an overarching word in place, it's now time to begin the process of setting and then reaching your goals in the season ahead.

There are "rules" to goal setting. You can do it right; you can do it wrong. We'll get into all that, I promise. But first, it's time to brainstorm. I want you to think of anything and everything under the sun that may or may not be a goal in your life. Then we'll prune them down. We'll separate the goals from the non-goals. We'll separate the dreams from the goals from the Words of the Year. We'll choose what's this year, and what's another year.

Let's ideate.

GET AN IDEAS NOTEBOOK

Goals start with ideas, and we need a lot of them.

We're about to go through a process that requires you to think big, and to have bold ideas about where you want to be. Think long and wide about the next few years ahead of you and what you want to do, accomplish, and feel in your work and your life. To do this, you'll need a lot of ideas.

Luckily, each one of us—whether we're teachers, doctors, mamas, programmers, businesspeople, tennis coaches, politicians, or cartoonists—has tons of ideas every day. Every hour, often. Every minute, sometimes. The challenge, however, is in effectively capturing those ideas.

When you have an idea in the shower, do you write it down? No. (Although SkyMall used to sell something to help you with that.) When you have an idea while tossing and turning at night, do you write that down? Not likely. When you have an idea in the subway, do you type it into your phone? Sometimes. The problem is not in coming up with the ideas, but in systematically documenting them.

So get a notebook. A tiny one. Not your regular hefty journal, and definitely not your phone. A real notebook you can touch and look at and think, *this is for all my terrible, horrible, no-good, very bad ideas.* (And some of the good ones as well.)

Carry it around. Use it *just for ideas.*

Don't listen to the part of your brain that says that you don't need one more notebook just to write down a random idea in. For years, I told myself I could use my regular journal. For years, it never worked. I didn't want to lug it around. If I did, I didn't want to take it out to write just one line in. It never worked until I designated one spot for just such content: a separate notebook *just* for ideas.

Get yours today.

BRAINSTORM

These days, that notebook isn't just going to be for incidental ideas. We're going to be actively courting them, and you'll need it to ideate on potential personal and professional goals you might want to pursue.

Brainstorming is a tricky art. Some folks can come up with five hundred mostly terrible ideas in fifteen seconds and some believe that ideas must be "good" before they see the light of day.

In *Applied Imagination: Principles and Procedures of Creative Problem Solving,* Alex Osborn set out the rules I follow when I brainstorm. Osborn's work holds that there are four basic tenets of brainstorming, and that they are important to ensuring that any brainstorming session results in positive, helpful ideas.

Here's how they work:

1. *Focus on Quantity:* Whoever said, "It's not quantity, it's quality," wasn't thinking about brainstorming. In brainstorming you want *as many ideas as possible.* This isn't always easy, so one way to do this is to motivate yourself by setting a specific number you want to come up with—say, twenty. Then, go a step further and commit yourself to coming up with those twenty ideas in a short period of time—five or ten minutes, say. This will help you to not overthink your ideas, and to keep on track with the next tenet.

2. *Withhold Criticism:* It's easy to think of this only being an issue when you brainstorm with someone else, or in a group setting, but in reality this is just as important when you're brainstorming by

yourself, since many of us are our own worst critics. Come up with a bad idea? Don't throw it out without writing it down. As Osborn's fourth tenet shows ("Combine and Improve Ideas"), even "bad" ideas can be tweaked to become great ideas.

3. *Welcome Unusual Ideas:* A similar concept to #2 (Withhold Criticism), the idea of welcoming unusual ideas is just to make sure that you are really thinking outside the box, and not limiting yourself to only "tame" ideas. Sure, some tame ideas might be great ones, but I'm willing to bet that most of the better ideas in your life (and mine) are the unusual ones. Also, as we'll see below, remember that often a wild and crazy idea can be the genesis of a fantastic (tamer) gem.

4. *Combine and Improve Ideas:* Your best idea isn't necessarily going to come fully formed to your brain. Instead, to really excel at brainstorming you've got to be ready to tweak, massage, and coax a great idea out of an okay or even poor idea. Combining and improving on ideas is essential to make this happen.

Ultimately, these tenets prove the point: with brain-storming, getting to good usually has to start with bad. So come up with lots and lots of bad, and, if you're like me, feel free to do so in gigantic sparkle-blue pen for added mirth.

FREEWRITE

Sitting down and asking your brain for a list of ideas is not always the best way to brainstorm, and many folks find that freewriting is a great way to supplement the brainstorming process to get that list of goals you need.

The act of freewriting is, in essence, the act of writing anything down without thought to what you're writing, why, or if it's even legible. The idea is that by writing out whatever you are thinking about, an idea will generate over time. Although people historically think of freewriting as a tool mainly for writers, Mark Levy's wonderful book *Accidental Genius* explains that anyone can use it as a powerful tool for ideation and idea generation.

Levy says there are a few key reasons for this.[1]

First, **freewriting gets the juices going and gets the writing and thinking process to flow**. The concept of getting your writing flowing is often the only reason most people think freewriting exists. And this is a good reason.

Freewriting *does* get the energy unblocked in your mind and gets your fingers clacking across the keyboard. But, critically, freewriting also gets the *thinking* juices flowing.

Second, **freewriting tells you what you know**. Are you having trouble coming up with any goals at all for the year ahead? Do you have way too many in your mind that you don't think are worth writing down? Are you not really sure what you want to focus on when thinking of potential goals—work or family? Are you simply baffled at where to start? Writing down what you do know is a key way to help you sort out your thoughts. If you start a brainstorming session and have no ideas, a ten-minute freewrite will induce some, guaranteed. By the same token, if you start a brainstorming session with lots of ideas you're not sure are fully fleshed out, a ten-minute freewriting session will help give clarity on which ones you really care about.

HOME IN: IS THIS A GOAL?

(Or is it a falafel?)

I don't mean to make fun of falafels. But I do have a saying.

If I'm at a restaurant, and I order lasagna, say, and it comes and I am taking my first bite and it doesn't taste like what it's supposed to taste like, I bring out my phrase: Is this a falafel?

It's the same with goals. You've come up with a whole host of words. But some of these aren't goals at all. They are falafels.

By now, you've written down a lot of ideas. You've ideated. Now it's time to take out those dozens and dozens of ideas and hold them up to the light. Shake them around. Look at them real good. And eventually distill them into your goals for the year (or season) ahead.

This is a process. It's *not* always linear, it's *often* messy, and it may or may not involve bulletproof coffee. (Coffee with butter. Yes, butter. Look it up!)

So, how can you start sorting out the goals from the falafels?

Goals, as we've all heard before, should first and foremost be actionable, and they should have a timeline. A goal is not "I want to make a billion dollars this year!"—unless you made 80 percent of that last year, of course, and a billion is actually a specific, reasonable number. A goal is something that you really can potentially achieve with a little sweat, grit, and (yes) luck thrown in.

Good goals must also have a timeline, or deadline. (The "line" at which said aim is "dead," if you will.) I certainly didn't create the concept of SMART goals, not by a long shot. Instead, a smart man named Paul Meyer did. According to Meyer, a SMART goal[2] is a goal that fits the following criteria:

• **SPECIFIC:** A goal should never be vague. For a few years now, I have set a goal to read two hundred books per year. This is not a vague goal. It is not "I want to read some books," or "I want to read dozens of books." No. I want to read two hundred books. A specific goal is specific. Period.

• **MEASURABLE:** It's not hard to measure a measurable goal—so find a goal you can count your progress against. If you are training for a 10K run, say, you need to plan out how many times you are going to run each week and for how many minutes. Three runs, twenty minutes each, say. Numbers are measurable. So are other things, but you get the point.

• **ACTIONABLE:** With an actionable goal, you know what to do next. If I want to finish my current book manuscript (I do), then I have a nifty word processing program called Microsoft Word I can go ahead and open up to get going. In fact, I can keep doing that every day for ninety minutes (or five hours, depending on the day!). Actionable goals tell you (or at least strongly hint at) what needs to happen next. To finish that book, I better fire up my MacBook Air.

Do you have a goal to expand your business? You've got to turn off House Hunters International and get cracking. Choose goals you can count progress against.

Although measurable goals don't need numbers attached, they do need a yardstick you can work against. They should not be things that will randomly be either done or not done come December 31. So if you have a goal to have one out-of-town family reunion this year with your extended family, you can reasonably guess that if in June you have not thought about this at all and neither has anyone else in the family, you are likely behind. Thinking creatively about ways to measure non-numeric goals is key.

• **RELEVANT:** Goals should be relevant to you and the year before you. Three years ago, health was top of mind for me, so I set a goal to try eating a thirty-day "Paleo" or Whole Foods diet. It's worked so well for me over the years that this year my goal is to eat 90 percent Paleo. Always make sure your goals are relevant to the particular season of life you are in. The year I had a baby, I decided it was not realistic to read two hundred books, and dropped my goal by 25 percent. (I heard that babies took up time. I heard right.)

• <u>TIMELY</u>: Goals must be timely. Let's say I want to write some ebooks, and I have a goal to self-publish two in a given year. It's best to put more of a timeline on that goal. The first book when? The second book when? Put a date by those numbers. And never forget important life events that aren't necessarily in your goals chart. If I have a goal to have at least one annual reunion with my college room-mates (I set this goal every year, and luckily it's a fun one to cross off), I should not plan for that to happen in the spring, when I have a baby due.

By understanding the SMART goals framework, we can now look back and see if the things we came up with during our brainstorming were actually goals, or if they were something else.

Take a look back at your list. If something doesn't fit the profile of a goal as outlined above, then is it a word of the year? Or a dream to think about later on? Or is it per-haps just an idea of something cool you'd like to do, but don't want to prioritize?

Sort all the ideas you came up with into three categories:

1. *A Word of the Year (or a Word of You)*: Your word of the year, as discussed, should be one defining word to help bring together what you wish to feel and accomplish in the year or season ahead.

2. *Dreams*: Your dreams should be big, bold ideas that you may want to pursue one day, but aren't ready to start actively working toward by prioritizing or putting a timeline on. If you're thirty, and you have dreams of retirement, say, or if you're eighteen and coaching your kids' little league games isn't around the corner.

3. *Goals*.

FINE-TUNING YOUR GOALS

"We overestimate what we can accomplish in a day, but underestimate what we can accomplish in a year."
—Chris Guilleabeau

At this point, you should have a list of goals that all fit the SMART goal framework. We now need to pare these down to a list that will work for you for this year.

One of the keys to goal setting is not to set too many of them. It can be easy for some folks to make a laundry list of things they'd like to accomplish that all meet the basic requirement of being a SMART goal. But it is not easy for most folks to accomplish every one of these goals. Ultimately, there is little worse in goal setting than getting 2 percent of the way through your massive list of annual goals, giving up, and throwing the whole list out with yesterday's recycling, never to be looked at again.

Keeping motivation high and your chances for success higher is essential, and doing so is dependent on not thinking too grandly about what can be accomplished. That said, I do not believe there is a specific number of goals you should set, and I don't stick to one number year in and year out. Instead, I (almost always) stick to the same categories.

Here's the concept: If you're going to live a life, you're going to have more than one goal to go after. Once you have multiple goals, categorizing them into areas of your life not only helps organize your thinking, but also helps take the pressure off of prioritizing one goal over another.

Let me explain: Many of my annual goals have more or less equal weight in my life, or at least fluctuate in their importance over the course of a year. Thus, putting goals into categories frees me up to choose a goal that might be "small" in one category of my life, and not worry that it's not equal to a goal that might be "large" in another category.

Let's see what this looks like in practice. Here are the categories I use for my goals most years, and the ones that many other folks find useful.

- God
- Family
- Health

- Personal
- Work
- Money

Within each of these categories, I have at least one goal each year, and often more than one. For some people who suggest that you should only have three to five goals a year, say, this may sound like a lot. After all, with six categories, just two in each means twelve goals a year. As I'll show, however, categorizing allows me to set "smaller" goals in some areas that do not require significant work on a daily basis, but are things I do want to be intentional about.

Let's look more deeply, using some of my goals in the past as examples.

GOD

When I got my first iPod back in 2006, I named my list of Christian music "God." This name has stuck. In this category I set goals related to my faith, which is the bedrock of everything else I do—the largest rock in the jar, and the one that goes in first. For me, this category often has to do with how I spend the time in my morning routine in terms of what types of books and devotionals I plan to read throughout the year.

Here are some examples:

- Read through the New Testament as a part of my morning routine.
- Read at least twenty books (as part of my larger reading goal) that guide or inform me in my faith.

FAMILY

For me, this is the category where my husband and I think about what we want to accomplish as a family this year. For example, last year I thought it was important to make two solo trips with my husband sans our glorious babe. I've also often set a goal to have one trip a year with extended family. So I set goals in this category like this:

- I want to take two solo trips with my husband this year.
- I want to do one extended family trip this year.

HEALTH

At times, like when I find a breath-o-meter on Kickstarter that promises to measure my hydration levels, I wonder if I've gone too far with the whole human guinea pig thing. (And then, I tap the sleep band on my wrist and fall asleep for exactly 9.5 hours like a baby.)

The health category is the place where my inner spreadsheet really shines, and where I take real advantage of the category system of goal setting to allow myself to set some goals that are about keeping me on track, and not producing or creating something.

In my health category, I think about what I want to do, and then I stick a timeline around it. Here are some examples from past years:

- I want to eat 90 percent Paleo this year. (This means about two or three non-Paleo meals a week. As I'll discuss, I use a simple app to check off when I eat non-Paleo meals, when I exercise, and when I do other things. This makes it easy to track.)
- I want to exercise an average of five out of seven days each week.
- I want to get a massage twice a month.
- I want to sleep an average of 9.5 hours a night.

PERSONAL

This is the category where I think of what I want to personally achieve that doesn't best fit elsewhere. Here are a few of the types of goals in this category:

- Do my morning routine (The Present Principle, which I'll explain later) an average of five out of seven days each week.
- Read two hundred books.

WORK

This is a big category, and there's always a lot in it, so I find that with this area in particular I need to really pare down and not overdo. I try to stick to the really important things.

Here are some examples from past years:

- Submit one book for publication this year.
- Publish thirty blog posts over the next twelve months.

MONEY

This is the category for setting goals for earning, saving, investing, and giving. When single and traveling the world for several years in my twenties, I was extremely frugal and very budget conscious, and began to write down everything I spent, thanks to the wise advice in the great book by Joe Dominguez and Vicki Robin, *Your Money or Your Life*.

Ultimately, this gave me a habit that has been hard to break—and it makes it easy to track financial goals. If that's not the case for you, I would encourage you to see what you're comfortable with in terms of ongoing financial tracking to help you meet your goals in this category.

Here is an example of one of my goals in this area from past years:

- Increase my giving by 10 percent over the next twelve months.

Now it's time for you to get started, and the first step is to create your categories.

Many folks use a version or variation on the ones I use above, so I believe they do serve as a good starting point. That said, some obvious other or substitute categories you might want to include are: Home, Parenting, Marriage, Extended Family, Nuclear Family, Giving, Church, Running, Sports, for example. Essentially you should think about the most important things in your life, and distill them into meaningful categories that work for you.

Once you have these in place, it's time to start placing goals into categories and evaluating where you stand. So, with a keen memory for catching those falafels, plug the remaining true "goals" into your chosen categories.

Now comes a critical, important test, and one of the hardest things you'll do in this entire process. It's time to ask yourself, honestly: **Do I have too many goals?**

As I explained, there are some folks who believe that a specific number of goals is important. *No more than five. No more than eight! Three is just right.*

I've never jumped on that bandwagon, though, and the most I can say for sure is that I do believe that having too many goals is a surefire way to lose focus. I'm not going to give you a number, but I will say this: Be realistic, and choose less rather than more. Also remember to think about the work involved with various goals.

For me, this is always most clear with my health goals. When I set a goal like, "eat 90% Paleo," it's not a goal that actually takes me more time or that I have to put in extra work or manpower to accomplish. I have to eat, and I have to shop for the food I eat no matter what kind of food I eat, so choosing this path simply replaces another one. Same with a goal like "read 20 books that relate to my faith." This goal, in terms of time, does not add to the goal "read 200 books this year." It just clarifies what my specific intention is within that larger goal, and writing it down on my list of goals that I regularly reference makes sure I will endeavor to hit it. That is not true, though, with a goal like, "submit one book for publication this year." I could easily spend my time doing a lot of things other than writing and publishing a book, and so setting this as a goal means that I must set aside time to do the work required to get it done.

Another key thing to remember is that some of your goals may be "fun" to work toward and execute, and others may be less so. This makes a difference when thinking of the overall number you can handle in a given year. For example, although I love my work, I find it more fun to read than work. So "publishing a book" will feel like more work to me than reading for pleasure will.

But that doesn't mean that all fun things are easy. Although vacationing with my extended family once a year may in and of itself be a fun experience, planning it is not easy, so I shouldn't discount the time it takes.

These are all critical points to think about as you analyze whether you have too many goals on your plate.

CREATE STRATEGIES TO REACH YOUR GOALS

Once you feel you have the right goals for your year ahead, it's time to dig deep into your goals and work out how to really accomplish them. One common goal on many people's lists is reading. Many of us want to read more, whether to become more informed on a given topic, or as a way to enjoy ourselves on a more regular basis.

But, as we've discussed, "read more" is not a very specific goal to go after. Putting a number on that goal is a great way to prioritize reading in a way you can really go after. Twelve is a good, round number, and a number on many lists of annual goals. Let's look at what a strategy would be like to ensure that you read twelve books this year.

BREAK DOWN THE GOAL

You don't hit a goal by doing it all at once, but by breaking it down. To read twelve books a year, you need to read one book a month, or one quarter of a book per week. If you stick to this average, you've got your annual goal covered. Some months you may not reach this, but some months (like when you go on vacation for a week and read a lot), you will exceed this.

FIGURE OUT HOW LONG IT WILL TAKE

Approximating how long a goal will take you to accomplish is key. In the case of reading, try timing yourself as you read to see how many minutes it takes for you to read one page. If we assume an average book has 250 pages, then you'll know how many hours (roughly!) it will take you to read an average book.

Let's say you find that it takes you about twelve hours to read one book. This means you need to read about three hours a week to hit your annual goal of reading twelve books. When you know these numbers, you can then face up to them with strategies to get that reading done.

The same works for any goal you set for yourself, whether it's running a marathon or increasing your giving by 10 percent or planning a vacation with family. Breaking down the goal into actionable items and determining how long it will take to accomplish that goal is essential. Sometimes this will be significantly easier than at other times. When faced with a goal like "self-publish a book," a thousand small tasks have to take place to make that happen. At this stage you don't need to have all those action items written down (or even know what they are yet!) but just plan as much as you can for the broad strokes of what needs to happen and when. Then you can move forward. At each stage of the larger process, you'll then again break down that part of the goal into smaller pieces. Once you know the steps you need to accomplish to reach your goal and you understand the time involved, you need to start employing strategies to reach your goal.

In the case of reading, for example, here are a few tactics you could use to read three hours each week:

READ TWO BOOKS AT ONCE

For some people, reading multiple books at once works wonders. By doing so, this means you never get bored of one book, and can always turn to whatever is most appealing in a given situation. In my own life, I know that if I have five minutes waiting in line, it's easier for me to read a memoir or novel than get through another page in a health or business book, for example. If I'm reading in bed late at night, I prefer dense nonfiction to help me fall asleep. Choosing different types of books on different occasions means that you'll be more likely to be "in the mood" for one of the books on your list.

AUDIOBOOKS CAN BE AN ESSENTIAL PART OF YOUR ARSENAL

I don't read every book with my own eyes, and neither should you. Using audiobooks is a great way to increase the time you can spend reading. I know someone who buys the print and audiobook version of a book so that she can switch back and forth between audiobook and print, depending on if she's in the car or at home. In my life, I have an audiobook going when I exercise, commute, get ready in the morning, do chores, or am doing anything else wherein an audiobook works as positive background noise.

PLAN WHAT YOU WILL READ

Some people swear by planning out what books they want to read each month or year. Crystal Paine, power blogger at MoneySavingMom.com, gives her readers lists of the books she wants to tackle in a given month. I find that I don't like being that precise, but I do have a few shelves of books just dedicated to books I want to get to some-time soon. I also have a list of books I want to read next in my email for those books I'll be listening to in audio-book or reading on Kindle. This means that any time I am ready to start a new book, I can easily see what books I've been itching to read and decide what feels right for the day or week ahead. This helps immensely to keep me motivated and excited.

Just as personal trainers say that setting out your run-ning clothes the evening before will make you more likely to go on your morning run, choosing the books you plan to read ahead of time can help motivate you.

ALWAYS BE ON THE LOOKOUT FOR NEW BOOKS

The desire to read is the biggest thing that will get you to actually do it, and that desire is built on there being a book that you want to *inhale*. So it's your job to make sure you're surrounding yourself with really good books, and not just mediocre ones. Keep a list of great books your friends or family recommend, and solicit suggestions from people whose opinions you value.

Further, think big and wide when it comes to books. For example, I'm a nonfiction or memoir girl at heart, and I have trouble remembering how freeing novels can be. Do you equate "reading books" with "reading boring business books"? If so, push yourself to go beyond the boundaries of your normal life. To feel better about your reading voyeurism, hit garage sales or mine Amazon.com for $.99 books. It'll encourage you to try new things without regret.

The same works for other goals as well. If you're trying to reach a goal, surrounding yourself with information, resources, or a relevant community in your daily life will increase your ability to hit it.

KEEP GOALS RELEVANT

One mistaken notion about goal setting is that you should always be incrementally increasing your goals. This "more is better" mindset is a trap I've fallen into many times before. In the past, I believed that if I hit my goal last year I should beat it this year. The reality, though, is that always increasing your goals can be just plain stupid, and can run in direct contrast to one of the keys in the SMART goal-setting framework: relevancy.

Smart goals must always be relevant to who you are in a given season of life. In my case, when faced with setting my annual goals for 2014, I had to come up against a very relevant reality of my upcoming 2014.

That reality? I was having a baby. And I was not the first person to have been told that babies take time, energy, and effort to keep in pristine, working order. As such, it made sense for me to think of this blaringly relevant life event when considering my list of potential goals. When I thought about where I could cut back, my goal to read two hundred books stood out as a bad idea. Although reading serves as my outlet, peacemaker, and primary hobby, it does take time to reach that goal, and time was at a premium for me that year.

As such, I reduced my 2014 reading goal to 150 books. And even though that's still a truckload of books, in some tiny way it did feel like I was throwing in the towel. After all, in my heart I really did feel like I could hit two hundred *if I just tried*. But is it smart goal setting to think of the relevancy of a goal in your particular season of life? Absolutely. The year 2014 just wasn't the one to stretch myself to read more. Remember to keep your goals relevant at all costs.

HOW DO YOU KNOW IF YOU
PICKED THE RIGHT GOALS?

One year, one of my health goals was about making sure I drank enough water each day. It sounds simple, and it is. Or that's what I thought. As soon as I wrote "drink the right amount of water" on my goals list, however, I stepped into a quagmire.

It turns out that there is a ton of conflicting advice online about how much water you should drink each day. Do you really need to drink half your weight in water? Or is it more like eight 8-oz glasses of water (which may be more or less than that, depending on your weight)? Does it really have to be all water? Or does tea count? Can homemade fruit juice or smoothies even be considered part of that number?

Twenty minutes of me, online, trying to figure out how much water I needed to drink, and I wanted to chuck the whole goal out the window.

This is ridiculous, I thought. *Who cares?* I wailed. (Me, apparently. Because who else spends twenty minutes cross-checking strangers' random responses to Yahoo Answer queries from 2009 as a means to determine anything about their health?)

Here's the thing: I never figured out the right answer. Today, I don't pretend to know the "right" answer or even if there is one. Instead, I just plowed ahead and picked a number. The goal I set (64 ounces a day) might be right. It might be wrong. But it's just what I chose. (And it happens to be exceedingly easy to remember, given that it makes up exactly two full bottles of the brand that I use.)

Sometimes, we're not always sure about the goals we set at the beginning of the year. Are they "right"? Are they wrong? Should they be different? If they aren't going to hurt you (drinking water shouldn't hurt me, I hear), then just try them. If they don't work, you can always change course.

KEEP YOUR
GOALS TOP
OF MIND

To stick to your goals, it's important to remember them—and not just a few times a year. We all need a regular reminder of what we're setting our sights on in order to get where we want to go.

Different people do this in different ways. One of the downsides of being married to a brilliant architect is that he has high standards about how things look in the lovely home he designed and built for us. As such, I have still not won the battle for a treadmill desk (he cannot think of something more aesthetically unappealing). Additionally, hanging a huge sign in my office with my chicken-scratched goals on it is not in his vision of aesthetic bliss. And that's okay with me. There are things on that list I'm not sure I want every houseguest to examine.

And for good reason.

One of my most cringe-worthy life memories relates to seeing someone else's goal list, in fact.

I was twenty and my friend Lara and I had gone to London to visit our friend Amalia. As I remember it, we experienced some classic travel nightmare in getting to England from Italy, where we were studying for six months. We missed a connection, a lot of running and sweat were involved, and we arrived exhausted and near delirious. Amalia's roommates were out of town that weekend, and they kindly let me and Lara sleep in their beds. When I tucked into the tiny twin in the turreted corner lent to me, I saw a list tacked up above my head. At first, I wasn't sure what I was looking at. And then I realized it was a list of goals.

I've tried to block out most of what happened next.

When I realized what I was seeing, I giggled. And then I started laughing. Hard. And then I told Lara to come over and she laughed. Hard. Pretty soon we were rolling on the floor making fun of the list. I don't even know what we laughed at, exactly. Whether it was the *idea* of the thing—tacking your goals on a wall! Ha! Or a *specific* goal in and of itself. Get good grades! Hysterical! Whatever it was, Amalia stopped us in our tracks, calling us out on our behavior. We immediately woke up to reality, apologized, and went to bed, embarrassed.

Even though I couldn't for the life of me tell you the name of the girl's bed I slept in that weekend, I've thought about this incident dozens of times in the years since. And although I'm sure no one who enters my house is one-tenth as mean as I was that night in London long ago, I'm still gun-shy about hanging my list up on a wall. Luckily, this works well with my husband.

My goals are in the front of my journal. Where I look at them daily. Find your place, and display them, proudly.

Now that you've got a word for your year, and some goals to work toward, it's time to live them.

PART TWO: ORGANIZE (LESS IS MORE)

"How we spend our days is, of course, how we spend our lives."
—Annie Dillard

We've talked about how to Decide on the key goals in your life, and now it's time to Organize your days to win.

Organizing your life, however, is not about taking a trip to the Container Store. Don't get me wrong; I love me a fancy fabric-covered box that promises to solve all my problems. However, I also know how ineffective it is in terms of long-term organization. To truly create an organized life and reach the goals you've set for yourself, the key is doing less. (The same holds for closets, it turns out. Less stuff is always the path to true organization.)

The Do Less Method offers that organizing well is a matter of four steps, and we'll go through these, point by point. The "O" (**Organize**) is divided into four parts. Each part makes up the word **LESS**.

L: LIMIT YOUR WORK TO YOUR BEST 20%

A massage therapist I know has spent her life around human bodies—strong ones, weak ones, and all the variations in between. She believes that the key to moving well is to listen to your body's desire to do less. Whether you're sitting in a chair or standing up tall, she says, you need to ask yourself how you can do less. Our bodies know that sitting on our sit bones, and not slouching, is better. Our bodies know that lifting something heavy works better when we squat and lift with all our power.

When I was pregnant with my daughter, this idea really hit home. For nine months, it felt like I wasn't doing much of anything. But really, while I sat in doctors' offices and lay around watching Agatha Christie movies—doing a whole lot of nothing, it felt like—the biggest thing I'd ever done was growing behind the scenes. More than anything, this was a reminder to me that we often don't realize when something truly powerful is taking place. Did that trip with a friend lay the groundwork for a new screenplay? Did the week off recharge your batteries to let you work well all season? In contrast, did your entire workday get sucked into a series of meetings that led to nothing? Did the volley of emails you sent back and forth this morning only add confusion—not clarity—to a situation at work? In everything we do, we need to think about when we are really making an impact, and always seek out the way to do less to do more.

When it comes to productivity, a key way to do this is to limit the things we do. The 80/20 Principle says that we accomplish 80 percent of our work in 20 percent of our time. Conversely, we waste 80 percent of our time spinning our wheels to get a measly 20 percent of our results. This means that to truly be productive we need to try and only do that 20 percent of things we are really good at that bring us great results, and eliminate the other 20 percent from our plate completely. Ultimately, this is the key to freeing up immense amounts of time and getting rid of those sixty-, fifty-, or even forty-hour workweeks.

If you can choose your hours or have control over how many hours you work, this concept is particularly revolutionary. Working in an office environment with fixed hours makes this more challenging, but there still are key ways to work in these lessons to make a powerful difference in your productivity and your life.

LEARN WHAT ONLY YOU CAN DO: DETERMINE YOUR "BEST 20%"

The first step is to identify those Best 20% activities.

Entrepreneur Chris Ducker is a great mind in the space of hiring outside help, and I've learned from him in developing my strategy to identify your Best 20% activities. This exercise will help you see where you should spend your time, where you should find resources or better delegate, and where you should work hard to simply stop doing a certain activity.

To get going, take out two pieces of paper. Label one BIG WINS and the other ACTIVITIES.

On the first sheet of paper, write down some of your biggest wins in the past few years in your personal and professional life. This should be a list of one-off individual things like, "The deal I closed with that big firm,"

"Appearing on my local radio station," "Taking a family trip to Mexico," and ongoing things like, "Learning from my mentor," "Taking piano classes," or "Spending regular time with my children."

On the second sheet of paper, ACTIVITIES, think about all the activities you take part in on a regular basis—no matter if they led to those big wins or not. Your list will include all manner of things: sleeping, eating, emailing, traveling, taking meetings, giving presentations, going to church, cleaning the house, spending time with kids, going to family events, commuting, attending Bible study, volunteering, etc.

Now, looking at the second sheet of paper, you need to identify which of three categories the things on the second sheet of paper fall into. Here are the three categories:

1. Things Only I Can Do: try putting stars around the "things only I can do" category, as these are the most important.
2. Things Someone Else Can Do
3. Things I Should Stop Doing

So, for example, "spending time with kids" does not fall under "Things Someone Else Can Do," as it is not something you can hire someone else to help you with, or something you can delegate to someone on your team. In contrast, cleaning the house is a great candidate for "Things Someone Else Can Do."

There might be some areas where one thing falls into two categories. For example, "traveling for work," although it is something only you can do, is not necessarily something you always need to do, or need to do as much as you do. Was that out-of-town meeting really necessary or did you just think you "should" be there in person? Could you have cut it out? Sometimes we think that all types of a certain activity are necessary, when we could pick and choose better and some instances might fall under "Things You Should Stop Doing."

Most people find that once you categorize the activities, it helps to rewrite them on a fresh sheet of paper into ordered columns of Things Only I Can Do (starred), Things Someone Else Can Do, and Things I Should Stop Doing. Once you're done categorizing them, it's now time to look back at the first sheet.

The first thing to do here is to look for where items on your Big Wins list also appear on your Activities list. The items that appear as Big Wins AND appear on the Activities List as "Things Only You Can Do" are your Best 20% Activities. Let's now order all the items on the Activities list to see where they fall in terms of your priorities.

• *First Priority: Big Wins + Things Only You Can Do*— These are your Best 20% activities and are key activities you need to prioritize in your life!

• *Second Priority: Big Wins + Things Someone Else Can Do*—These are important activities you need to keep doing, but they are things you need to delegate to someone else to do. Whether that means hiring a part-time assistant or mother's helper a few hours a week, or working to delegate better at work, you need to work hard to protect your time to not personally take on these activities.

• *Third Priority: Things Only You Can Do*—Evaluate carefully the activities here, because they are not on your list of Big Wins. Some, you will see, you may need to continue. Some, you do not. Challenge yourself to also think broadly about what this means.

• *Not a Priority: Things You Should Stop Doing*— Try to stop doing these activities as much as possible.

Let's look more in-depth into each priority category.

First Priority:
Big Wins + Things Only You Can Do

First and foremost, you need to make sure to think hard about these first-priority items—after all, they will get top billing. If you put on your ACTIVITIES list that speaking at conferences is something that only you can do, you then need to 100 percent ensure that speaking at conferences is actually a Big Win for you, and that it's not just on the Big Wins list because it sounds impressive or others would be eager to do it.

Additionally, it's also important to think about what steps really contribute to your big wins. If speaking at conferences on the surface doesn't seem like a Big Win in and of itself (say, you aren't getting paid enough for it to make a big difference in your household income, or it's very tiring), then how important is it to helping you get clients, for example? If it's only somewhat important, is there another way you can achieve the same result with less time invested?

Second Priority:
Big Wins + Things Someone Else Can Do

Some of the activities on your list are not things that only you can do, but are activities that directly contribute to your big wins. For example, a blogger might find that posting regularly on social media is important to driving traffic to her website, but in reality those posts aren't personal posts and thus don't need to be done by the blogger herself.

When this is the case, the most important thing you can do is delegate this activity out to someone else. Finding help is absolutely critical to ensuring you do your best work. If you work in a larger organization and don't have the ability or authority to get an extra set of hands, then the key for you is to make sure that you aren't taking on tasks or activities that are really the role of someone else. If you do work for yourself and have the autonomy to hire help or have money in your family budget to help out your family at home, start to understand that the investment you make in hiring someone to do these activities will pay itself back in the time you earn to do your best work (which will, ultimately, earn you more time and happiness).

Third Priority:
Things Only You Can Do

This category is full of some important things that we need to do every day (sleep, eat, groom, go to the dentist) that you might not think contribute to your Big Wins, and many, many things that regularly drain our time. Some people, for example, are quick to say that only they can manage their calendar, book their flights, clean the house, make the dinners, cut the grass, or drive the carpool, but if they think really broadly, they might see they could hire someone to help.

Additionally, if you put on your list that attending meetings is something that only you can do, you're likely right—most of the time. Additionally (and unfortunately!), most meetings do not directly contribute to great results and 99.9 percent will not appear on your list of Big Wins. In this case, the best you can do is limit your involvement to the greatest extent possible.

Not a Priority:
Things You Should Stop Doing

Many of us have things we know we "shouldn't be doing." This is your chance to get rid of those activities, once and for all.

Additionally, though, it is essential in this category to not cut out all your meaningless activities. The #1 thing people forget to put on their Big Wins list is relaxing or rest. The reality is that we all need downtime desperately in order to be truly productive—and I believe that it is only when we are truly rested (and I don't just mean sleep) that our bodies naturally upswing into productivity. If this isn't a reason to rest, I don't know what is.

You absolutely need to keep some of your fun, non-productive activities on that list. No, you don't need to watch the American average of five hours of TV each day.[3] (And if you do now, you should absolutely make some of that time "Not a Priority: Stop Doing," but yes, you may be someone who enjoys and benefits from watching a good movie on the weekends to relax.)

Ultimately, this activity is a mind-opening way to see where your time and work is really moving the needle, and where you're just running on the hamster wheel to stay busy.

SAY NO

Saying NO is one of the hardest things many of us have to do on a regular basis. Unfortunately, it's also one of the best, and it's absolutely critical if we are trying to limit ourselves to our Best 20% that we learn how to say no, and do so frequently. As Lysa Terkeurst says in *The Best Yes*, "Whenever you say yes to something, there is less of you for something else. Make sure your yes is worth the less."

It's true. A chain of *no* responses paves the way for powerful yeses, and ultimate success.

E: EDIT THE TIME YOU SPEND ON WORK

"Work expands so as to fill the time available for its completion."
—Parkinson's Law

Tim Ferriss, author of *The 4-Hour Workweek*, became famous for telling us that we could only work four hours a week and still succeed. And although his book's title isn't exactly literal, the overarching concept is true: we can absolutely work less and win. In fact, as I believe, working less is a key way *to* succeed. Tim believes combining two distinct concepts is essential to working less. Specifically, the 80/20 Principle (that we spend 20% of our time to do our best 80%) and Parkinson's Law (that work expands to fill the time we have to complete it).

And Tim Ferriss is hardly the only one who thinks this works. Author and international development consultant William Powers says that by layering these two concepts over one another he was able to take his five-day workweek down to two days. Alongside the other tools in the Do Less Method, this is how I do my work and read and sleep more than most people I know.

Let's explore the specifics of editing the time you spend on your work.

TRACK YOUR TIME

To edit down the time you spend on work, you first need to know how much time you're spending on the things you do. This is an important exercise, and there are a few good ways to do this:

A Notebook or Excel Spreadsheet

Time experts like Laura Vanderkam might say that there's nothing better than a good old grid for a true time diary (whether in an Excel spreadsheet or on graph paper). The concept is simple: divide the day into twenty-four hours. Spend a week or a month noting what you do during the course of a twenty-four-hour period and add up the results to understand where you spend your time.

That said, there are also some online tools I swear by to step in and smooth out the process.

Rescue Time

RescueTime is a program that automatically tracks all the time you spend on the computer, giving you a report at the end of the week (or day) showing exactly what you were doing every minute of every day that your computer was on. It can also track any off-screen time you manually input. It also has functionality to help you hit and reach productivity goals—like helping remind you not to spend more than 40 percent of your workweek in your email inbox.[4]

Moment

Remember that your digital work time doesn't just happen on your computer, and that you likely spend far more time on your mobile device each day than you think. Moment is a great app that tracks how much time that really is. It doesn't break it down into categories like Rescue Time, but it does tell you how many minutes you've been on your phone each day, and can also help remind you to stay off it if you go over your prescribed goals.

More than just knowing where you are spending your time, many tools can help you track some of the overarching goals you've set for yourself. Here are a few:

An Activity-Tracking Device

There are a number of different wearable devices on the market, and I've tried a few. Whatever tool you use, though, the idea is to track sleep, exercise, steps taken, and potentially heart rate to get a better sense of your overall health metrics, and to work toward bettering yourself. These tools will provide data that will not only give a detailed picture of how you spend your time, but will also help you stay on track to hit any health goals.

Coach.me (or another Habit-Tracking App)

Although the Coach.me app can be used to help show how you spend your days, it is most helpful as a way to track the goals you're checking off on a daily basis. Meaning that it works best for regular goals—so not "go on two solo vacations with my spouse this year," but rather, "eat fish three times this week," or "get a massage twice a month." I have a few of my goals set up and every time I do one of my goals, I check in and it adds up over time. You can also see who else in the world hit the same goal that day as well.

Ultimately, the idea is not only to track how you spend your days, but also to understand how long it takes you to do those regular activities that make up your Best 20%. If you're a writer, say, knowing how long it takes to write a blog post, or approximately how long it will take you to write a magazine article or book, is really important information. The same goes for anything in your work life. Over time, this will give you key information.

REDUCE THE TIME YOU SPEND ON YOUR WORK

The biggest misconception people have about working less is that you'll get less done. In reality, if you made yourself work twenty hours this week instead of forty, you would likely adjust quickly to identifying what is important, and to only doing those things. This is the premise behind the concept of editing down the time you spend at work.

Once you've tracked your time for a few weeks and know where you are spending your time, you are ready to tackle the task of editing down the time you're spending on your work. By doing this after you have started the process of trying to only do your Best 20% work, you should be able to fluidly start seeing some early results.

Here are some key ways to start seeing progress in working fewer hours:

Keep Strict Work Hours

I wasn't the only one in Silicon Valley who breathed a sigh of relief when Sheryl Sandberg went public saying she always leaves the office at 5:30 p.m. every day.[5] Keeping strict office hours, even in a Silicon Valley company where the doors can be open 24/7, is a key strategy for those in an office environment to consider, and I highly recommend working toward achieving this. From my years in Silicon Valley I know firsthand how hard it is to deal with the expectations of other team members who are happy to sit in their seats working (unproductively) for fourteen hours at a stretch, but remember that your health and sanity may depend on it.

In my case, I knew I regularly slept several hours longer than most of my colleagues, so working more than ten hours in my Silicon Valley office on top of commute time simply was not an option in order for me to get the sleep I needed. As a result, I was intentional about working more productively. Ultimately, if you work in an environment where clear business hours are not expected, it is important to create your own boundaries.

In graduate school, for example, I had a professor who set an auto-responder that explained when her working hours were, and when they weren't. If you emailed at the wrong time of day or night, you simply could not expect a response until her next window of time opened up. She claimed that this single act alone had saved her sanity and she felt free from expectations to work outside of these hours, because she simply told people she would not be available.

Jessica Turner, author of *The Fringe Hours*, has a full-time job in marketing but also has a host of other interests and hobbies. In order to pursue her passions, she learned years ago it was essential she use her "fringe hours" outside of work and family time wisely. And she did. As her husband says, she can get more done from five to nine in the morning than most people do between nine and five!

For those who work for themselves, keeping strict work hours is an essential step that is often overlooked. Crystal Paine, author of *Say Goodbye to Survival Mode*, works hard to ensure her computer is turned off by 6 p.m. at night—no matter what. For a work-at-home entrepreneur like Paine, this is more important than ever, since working for yourself tends to blur the barriers between work and everything else. This is especially important when you love your work. Author and blogger Ruth Soukup fervently loves her work—and says happily that she would be fine working seven days a week. That said, this year she promised her husband she would take every Sunday off. I bet it will be one of the best things she does for her productivity.

Go on a Work Diet

In *New Slow City*, author and consultant William Powers commits to trying to work only two days a week for a year. It's a radical experiment, and one that pays off in spades. Week after week, he finds that he's able to get done what could take five days in just two, squeezing forty hours of unproductive work into sixteen hours of true productivity. When, midway through his year, he adds to his schedule by accepting a professorship, he experiences the challenges of balancing the goal to work less with new, outside expectations for longer, sometimes unproductive hours. Ultimately, though, he is able to succeed at working less than five days a week by remembering all he learned when taking time into his own hands.

I have tried many of my own experiments with this over the years, while both employed by organizations and when working for myself. Some of those include: not working more than twenty hours a week (highly effective when I was self-employed); doing three months' worth of writing projects in one solo weekend (very effective); only working five hours a week on an extended vacation and seeing if I could stay head above water (mostly, but hard); testing how two days offline over the weekend changes my Monday efficiency (it vastly improves it); and testing how a twelve-day period offline changes my productivity upon return (another great improvement).

Ultimately only you can decide what is right in your situation. The goal is to challenge yourself to place strict boundaries around your work responsibilities, and try to drastically reduce the time that you actually spend on them. Experiment to see what you can do in your own life to reach this aim.

Find an Organization That Cares about Results

Finding an organization that embraces a Results-Only-Work-Environment (ROWE),[6] where employees are evaluated on performance, not presence; asking to spend more time working remotely (where you can save hours a day on commuting and office socializing); or trying to make a long-term switch to working for yourself are also key thoughts to pursue.

If these bold ideas aren't realistic short-term options and you are employed with an organization that isn't helpful in your attempts to more productively manage your time, try to see if you can make any headway encouraging change from within. It's hard to convince a whole organization to follow suit in editing down the hours worked, but it is possible. I have friends who work for a publishing house in Michigan that has a "summer hours" policy. In the summer, employees come in earlier, leave earlier, and take off half of Friday to go home and be with their families. I loved this idea, and when I asked why they did it, they looked at me blankly. "It's summer in Michigan!" they said. "We only get this weather for a few months a year—and we need to enjoy it." To them, it was obvious. To me, it was revolutionary. By enjoying their summer, they'll surely be more rejuvenated and work better all year long.

S: STREAMLINE THE WORK YOU DO

HACK YOUR MORNING

The power of creating a positive morning routine that sets your day up for success cannot be stressed highly enough, and I'm a raging fan.

Importantly, it's hard to talk about a morning routine without giving a nod to the idea of actually waking up earlier.

We've all heard the rumbling about morning people: *Morning people get more done. Morning people are more effective at everything they do. Morning people win more often.*

The world might as well come clean and say what it really means: *Morning people do better in life.* The reality is that morning people do seem to get an awful lot done, and even night owls have reported that waking up early in the morning can make them feel more productive and more content with the work accomplished. As an experiment, try it out for yourself (this is easy if you work for yourself, but if you work for others you'll have to vary this experiment up to perhaps include a weekend day to understand its purpose).

Work for only three hours tomorrow, and do it at 8 a.m. Then, the next day, start your work at 4 p.m. At the end of each day, think of how productive you felt. Chances are, the day you started work in the afternoon will have left you feeling behind all day—even when you put in the same number of work hours.

I'm naturally a late chronotype (or "night owl" for you animal lovers), and I need more sleep than most people I know, so I've spent a lot of time trying to figure out how to regularly wake up earlier. One of the first things I realized in my attempts to hack my mornings was that I was going to be tired at first. And, if you're like me and you travel across time zones with some frequency, this isn't a one-time thing. You will be tired every time you try to force your body to wake up earlier. Luckily, it's a short-term loss for a long-term gain.

DEVELOP A MORNING ROUTINE

Getting up earlier isn't all you need to set yourself up to win. After all, it matters immensely what you do in that morning time. Some years ago I started implementing a seven-step process I have come to call the Present Principle. This is a simple routine built around the acronym PRESENT, which helps me remember to implement the seven most important things I need to do each and every day to keep me present in my life—and to do those things in the mornings.

Here's an overview of my routine. Remember that this is what works for me, and that you may not like all the steps at hand. Just ignore what doesn't work for you, and always work toward the goal of finding something that sets *your* day up for success.

Ultimately, this takes me about twenty to thirty minutes each day, and I often find myself reflecting that it is the single best thing I do to start my day well.

In brief, the letters stand for:

Pray (for guidance, direction)
Read (usually something scriptural or devotional)
Express (put your thoughts on paper)

Schedule (sketch out an overview of the day)
Exercise (you'll feel better when you move daily!)
Nourish (do something for yourself)
Track (at the end of the day, track your progress
in how much of your routine you were able to
accomplish)

(You can read more about this in my book *The Better Life* or at ClaireDiazOrtiz.com.)

Some days you won't do every step, and sometimes you won't do any of them. But trying to implement a routine such as this can be a powerful motivator.

ORDER YOUR DAY TO WIN

Writing, like dozens of other things people do each and every day, is a task that requires focus and concentration, and a task that usually requires your best work.

I'm an efficient writer and have always enjoyed being able to write quickly. That said, it's critical that I know when I can write well and when I can't. Because if I write when I'm not working well, I've no hope of efficient writing, and every hope of extreme frustration.

The other day, for example, I went to a coffee shop where I was going to spend a few hours writing. I know for sure that it's easier for me to write outside of my home office. Writing at a coffee shop generally works for me, and I can plow through quickly to get a lot done.

But not that day.

That day, I arrived. I sat down on the couch I'm a fan of. I ordered a freshly squeezed orange juice. I pulled out the computer. And that's where it went downhill. Somewhere between checking email, and then checking Twitter, and then rechecking email, and then reading an interesting article, I got all lost and tangled up. Pretty soon I was texting my husband, José: *When are we going grocery shopping? Now, please?*

Because I would rather go grocery shopping than write. Obviously.

In order to work well, you need to know when you are most effective and utilize those times to do your work. I would go further and say you don't just need to know when you're effective, you need to know when you are most effective for the specific task at hand. And so the fact that I wandered into the coffee shop on a holiday at 3 p.m. was never going to turn out well. I do my best writing in the morning, with a large decaf coffee with almond milk or after dinner, with a cool Kombucha. These are times I can write. The afternoon is not my writing time.

We all have times of the day and days of the week that work best for particular tasks, and it is essential to figure out what those times are and to make sure that we respect them to their holiest extent.

When José picked me up to go grocery shopping, I felt icky and annoyed. I had done very little work, and most of it was terrible. The wrong time of day, you see. I'd bungled it all up from the start and needed to remember my own rule. Only work when you can work well.

THE POWER OF FOCUS AND DECISION FATIGUE

If you're reading this book, I'm betting this isn't your first rodeo. You've probably read something about productivity and goal setting before, and if so, you've likely heard the now-common advice to **do the hard thing first thing**. Brian Tracy, author of *Eat that Frog!*, is one of the biggest proponents of this strategy, and his teachings have done much to convince folks that doing hard things first thing is essential.

Got an important memo to write? Do it first thing. Got a mission-critical presentation to finish? Do it in the morning before anything else.

That said, most folks don't actually remember why this is so important. It turns out it's not just about the fact that morning folks are more productive or about the fact that finishing one task helps you feel more productive and encourages you to keep going. Instead, I believe the key reason that doing the hard thing first thing is a good idea is all about warding off the energy-zapping power of decision fatigue and maximizing your energy to focus.

Listen up:

The reason you need to do your big job in the morning is that you will always have the most energy to focus *before* you get decision fatigue.

New to the term *decision fatigue*? Decision fatigue is that vitality-draining experience you get after spending an hour trying to decide on the best flight home to your parents' house for Thanksgiving weekend (wake up early on Monday morning to fly home? Or pay more to fly back Sunday night?), or why you feel tired after an hour at the paint store trying to figure out what color to paint your bathroom (periwinkle? teal? cyan?). It's even the reason why some life-hacking entrepreneurs swear by wearing the same thing each day, or eating the same thing for lunch! Decision fatigue is the exhaustion you get from making decisions, and it takes a real and present toll on our daily productivity.

By the same token, doing your hard thing requires

focus. I believe that one of the biggest reasons we procrastinate on our big work and spend far too much time in email and meetings during our work days is because when we lack focus, we do the thing that doesn't require that much focus at all. Email, it turns out, is a great candidate for that—so one of the great reasons to not get engaged in email first thing is to keep your mind energetic for your big task. Meetings can also fill time on doing things that don't require your maximum focus. Doing hard work, it turns out, requires focus. You will always be most energetic, and most likely to focus, before decision fatigue sets in. Although I'm betting you'll be more energetic earlier in the day, let's find out for sure.

WHEN IS THE RIGHT TIME OF DAY TO WORK?

My try-hard-do-little day at the coffee shop attempting to churn out some writing was an abject failure. Despite the fact that I am generally someone who can put pen to paper with particular speed, that day I did nothing of the kind.

But what I did do that day was confirm, once again, how important it is to know the time of day I'm best at a host of regular activities in my life.

Things like:

Exercising
Relaxing (yes! There is a time of day for this!)
Leading meetings
Taking conference calls
Giving presentations
Doing my daily PRESENT time
Emailing
Brainstorming
Doing research
Chatting on the phone with family and friends
Having difficult conversations
Reading

If you want to work toward having more productive days, it is essential to figure out the best times of days to do the activities that either make up your Best 20%, or are otherwise required for you and your family to live a great life, and then to build a loose schedule around it. You won't be able to choose things perfectly, but trying to create your schedule around your best times—and knowing why something isn't working well if it's out of order—is just as essential.

Here are a few steps to try to build these better lives we're after using this strategy:

1. Refer to your ACTIVITIES list and look at all the items in the "First Priority: Best 20%" column and the "Third Priority: Things Only I Can Do" column—so, the two columns of ACTIVITIES made up of things that you personally are going to keep doing on a regular basis.

2. Now *think* about when you're best at each of those things. *Really think.* Don't answer right away, but rather take some time to think about it. If an answer doesn't come, keep watching to notice how you behave at different times of day, and how certain activities sit with you. It took me a long time to realize, for example, that attending meetings was a far better use of my lower energy afternoon time than leading presentations, which for me was best in the morning. Watch yourself as you live your life, and think about it, over time. Remember the importance of the Power of Focus and Decision Fatigue when deciding these times, as most people's Best 20% activities likely need that high-energy time before decision fatigue takes away their powers.

Slowly but surely, you can **start to build a life designed around living at the right time of day for you**. Even if you aren't someone with a detailed schedule day in and day out, this can still work incredibly to give you the broad-strokes picture of how you should run your days.

KNOW WHEN TO STOP FORCING YOURSELF

Learning about what time of day you are best suited to do specific work is essential. But there's a corollary lesson that is also important to learn: **Sometimes, it's best to stop working**.

Or, sometimes it's best to stop forcing yourself to do work you're not doing well. In the story I told you, about me at the cafe not doing the writing I was supposed to be there for, I left out an important detail. That detail is the moment I realized that I needed to stop trying. All our lives, we hear again and again about the importance of not giving up. Truth be told, though, most of the advice we receive about the importance of trying hard is not that useful.

Because, in reality, **we all need to know when to stop trying**.

And I don't mean in some large sense of the word—when to quit a job, when to put down a project, when to admit something has truly failed. That's a very valuable thing as well, but right now I'm just talking about the importance of knowing when to stop trying on any given day when you're in the middle of a particular project or activity.

For me, the answer is all about flow.

In certain types of work I do, flow is critical. Otherwise known as "the zone", this popular positive psychology term named by Mihály Csíkszentmihályi is the mental state when you are completely immersed in what you are doing with intense focus and energized engagement. Writing, for example. Brainstorming, for sure. The act of creation in general, often. Most people report that these tasks go better when they're in the zone. And most of us know very intimately when we feel like we're there, and when we feel like we're not.

The reality is, when you're not in a state of flow, it's rarely going to be to your benefit in terms of time effectiveness to keep going. Now, often that doesn't matter. Say you have a presentation to prepare for in three hours' time and you're not feeling the flow. Too bad. Keep working. But if you do have a choice, that's when you can really make headway. Take the example of writing. If I am in a productive state of flow, I can crank out in two hours something that might otherwise take five.

The same goes for a host of other activities—from doing a spreadsheet to building a house to producing a podcast.

Ultimately, the key to doing your best work in the least amount of time is to find those times that you do specific activities best, and do as much of those activities in that time period as possible.

KNOW WHEN TO JUST DO IT

Sometimes, you've just got to sit down and do the work. In Ann Patchett's memoir, *This Is the Story of a Happy Marriage*, she talks about how to make yourself write when you don't want to. As Patchett says, **you've got to show up**. You've got to sit yourself down at your desk for two hours each day without books to distract you, or an open Internet connection. *You've just got to sit there.* Doing nothing. And after a week—or maybe two—you will either start writing because you are so bored out of your mind from not writing, or you will get up out of the chair, go watch television, and never write again.

Now, I believe this advice is not limited to writing, and in reality works for anything you're trying to do. Are you trying to make yourself do the one thing on your list that you never get to because you'd rather come up with a million excuses for how busy you are or how many useless errands you have to run?

Here's what you need to do: Sit yourself in the chair and

do nothing. At the right time of day when you know you should be productive. Day after day. *Until you do that thing.*

It's worth a try.

And not just for writers.

BATCH WORK

One powerful concept that is essential to add to your productivity arsenal is to make sure you are batching your work. Most individuals do a number of different things in any given hour of the day, with no regard to the fact that switching back and forth between activities—calls, emails, writing memos, coding, doing design layout— takes a huge toll on our productivity. In fact, studies show that we lose up to 40 percent of our time in any given day by switching back and forth between tasks.[7] You can reap huge rewards and make yourself infinitely more productive by batching your work to do similar tasks in bulk.

For example, I work hard to keep my meetings and calls batched into certain days of the week and times of day, and my creation days batched into others (this also addresses the issue that creation tasks require more focus). So, for example, if you determine you have about fifteen hours of meetings a week for work, you would try to schedule those as much as possible to fit within two or three days. Especially when working within a large organization, this requires you to make an art of calendaring your meetings well, but as I've seen even within the busy meeting environment of Silicon Valley, it is very possible, and it pays off remarkably.

This works for all manner of tasks, and you'll likely find that most of the things on your ACTIVITIES list will work within this strategy—from running errands, to going to doctors' appointments, to managing email, to doing creation-based work.

As I'll talk about further, I make sure to also process email in batch as well, another huge time-saver.

PUT IT ON THE CALENDAR

My friend Erik Fisher has a podcast called "Beyond the To-Do List." When I first heard about this podcast, I thought Erik had drilled into my brain to create it, as I can't think of anything more fascinating than spending half an hour a week listening to how other people try to be productive. One time when I was on his podcast, he was talking about how to use a calendar smartly. Erik told me that Jerry Seinfeld has said that he became a better joke writer by ensuring that he wrote a joke each and every day. To maintain this discipline he used a calendar with the whole year on one page, and he hung it on a wall where he would always see it. Whenever he did his work for the day, he'd use a big red marker to check off that he'd completed his task.

Some folks say that if it's not on your calendar it won't get done. I agree, and tell folks to calendar as much as you can to encourage yourself to do what you need to do. This is most essential, I find, when talking about things you wouldn't normally think to block off time for on a calendar.

Like your, ahem, work.

Let me explain:

In your work life, you likely spend 40 percent of your time on email.[8] If you work in an organization with other employees, you probably spend 35–50 percent of your time in meetings.[9] In a forty-hour workweek, this means that you might have as little as four hours a week to do the rest of your work!

The only way to get this done in this day and age (aside from editing what you need to do, as we've discussed) is to be sacred with your time, and sacred with your calendar. Keep appointments with yourself to "work" as religiously as you keep appointments with your boss. Finally, make sure that you batch similar activities into similar blocks of time.

TAME YOUR EMAIL

At face value it seems like email is the biggest blow to productivity the world has ever seen. But first impressions can be deceiving.

The reality is that emailing is necessary to our work lives, and we need to email to succeed in our careers. We are expected to exchange emails with clients, partners, and coworkers, and to do so in a timely manner.

Furthermore, since email is not something that can just be "fit in" at the end of the day around "real" work, we need to acknowledge the massive amount of time we spend on this task and make it a part of our work hours. So, if you wondered why you didn't feel restored after your Sunday "off," consider how that ninety minutes of emailing factored into things.

That said, email is a special kind of work.

The vast majority of email is not creation-based and does not lead to tangible results. Email doesn't write a book or a record a song or cook a gourmet meal for thirty. Hundreds of emails strung together do not lead up to a finished project. Instead, email is a fishbowl of semi-distracted people pinging each other back and forth ad infinitum. As Jon Acuff likes to joke, can you ever be done with the Internet? Do you ever log off and say, "Yup! I finished the Internet today"?

In a word? No.

Same thing goes for email.

You will never be done with email. Someone will always want to ask you to do something. Someone will always want you to get back to them about something. Someone will always be in your inbox, waiting for you to respond yesterday.

So, given all this, how do we go about managing it? How do we acknowledge that it is necessary to do deals, write books, and communicate with communicators, but keep it from getting in the way of creation? Specifically, how do we figure out a productive system to best respond to emails?

First, I believe that 95 percent of the time email does not require the same level of energy as our other projects do. And so I agree with folks who say that you should never email first thing in the morning. Instead, with those first few hours of peak energy that most of us have before decision fatigue sets in, we should focus on our most difficult task of the day, and get that done. This is not a new idea, and it appears in many other books on productivity. Although there are always exceptions—writer

Gretchen Rubin, for example, likes starting her days with an hour of email and social media because she finds it energizing—for the vast majority of people email is an energy suck, and should not be the first thing you do when you sit down at your desk.

That said, telling you when *not* to email isn't suggesting when you *should* respond to emails. So when is it best to respond to emails, if not in the first few hours of the morning when you first turn on your computer?

I believe there are a few key times when it's best to do real emailing. And by "real emailing" I mean when you spend a chunk of time devoted to working through a bunch of emails, and not when you send a one-off urgent response to something from your iPhone or from your computer while you're typing furiously in a Word document to meet a deadline in another screen.

Here are some email rules to live by:

• *As much as possible, email should be done in bulk.* There are always exceptions to this rule, but in order to be truly productive you need to slot the bulk of your emailing into specific times of the day—and not too many times! The alternative, which most of us fall into the trap of, is doing our "real" work all day with email perpetually pinging in the background, ready to interrupt our concentration and derail us on a near-constant basis, even for the most minor of queries or cute cat pictures.

• *Email should be done when you have less energy, rather than more*. Figure out when that is, whenever it is, and create a block of time in your schedule to fit in your emailing in that period. In my experience, the lull in the afternoon is a great time to go through a bunch of non-urgent emails.

I recommend thinking about your email in terms of four categories:

- Urgent
- Daily
- Weekly
- Never

In my email inbox, urgent and daily emails generally come from the same sources, and the response time is simply determined by the degree of urgency I associate with the particular note at hand.

Here is what this category of email is mostly made up of:

Urgent and Daily Emails

• *"Live" projects*: In the course of a year in your chosen profession, you might have fifteen projects on your plate (just go with this number for this example—your number may be different). In the course of any given month in that year, you might be in some stage of development/analysis with up to six of those individual projects. However, only a few of those will be considered "live" at any given time. These two or three live projects will get top billing in that month—meaning that the majority of your attention will be focused on them. Sure, you might think of and respond to notes about some of the other projects—but it is the "live" ones that you are most attuned to.

• *Life-changers*: This is a mixed bag. Generally, though, life-changers are some type of make-or-break news (you sold your company! the IRS is auditing you! your mother's participating in a flash mob!) or opportunity (a significant press opportunity! a president wants to meet you!). You know these when you see them.

• *Inner circle emails*: We all have one of these circles, and these folks get top billing, even when they are emailing their tenth pregnant stomach shot or stupid animal YouTube clip this week. To be a happy individual connected to friends and family, this is healthy and important (and not unproductive).

Weekly emails

I consider weekly emails to generally be emails that are often about other people's agendas. Typically, these are queries from people who want things I may or may not be able to give that are not considered urgent, and do not fall into any set of my real priorities. These are emails I do want to respond to, but should not do on a daily basis if I hope to get my own work done.

Never Emails

We all know what these are, and have different standards for what these may be. I believe that email can become even more challenging when you face a regular stream of *unsolicited emails*. These are emails from folks you don't know who want things, want to tell you things, want to ask you things, or want to yell at you about things (see more on that last one below).

As someone with an active online life and a popular blog, I get a lot of these unsolicited emails. And, for years, I tried hard to respond to many of the ones I get.

But there was always one type of email I tried to never respond to. I called it the Toxic I Hate You Email.

Is there an email sitting in your inbox that screams at you for something you likely never did? An email that bashes you for something someone read about you that isn't even true? An email that makes inaccurate assumptions about your life and then cuts you down for them?

My advice: just don't respond. It's not worth your time.

In 2006, when I first started a blog, and random people online who didn't know me were able to contact me for the first time in my life, I started learning this lesson. Years later, I'm still at it. I'm not perfect, and I mess up. Just this month, I responded to one because it was so appallingly offensive. The result? I started an idiotic chain of toxic emails that took up my headspace for a few of my short hours on this planet.

Was it stupid? Highly. Did I regret it? Very much so. How did it end? I stopped responding and put a filter in Gmail to immediately trash all future emails from the person. (If I didn't do this, I knew I'd be tempted to keep at it!)

The lesson is simple. Get an insanely negative email in your inbox from someone you don't know about something you're not responsible for? Don't answer. Unless you want to feed a troll. Then go ahead and respond. Spend your energy trying to convince someone of something they'll never be convinced of. Start an email war. But I don't recommend it.

What do I recommend?

Think boundaries, and don't invite crazy in.

An Email System That Works

- Check your email daily to deal with urgent and daily emails.
- Every week, calendar aside time to deal with weekly emails in one fell, focused swoop.
- Never deal with never emails.

MEETINGS

People who have worked with me know how much I dislike meetings, and how I've made something of a study of figuring out why our meeting culture is so broken. When the reality is that we spend 35–50 percent of our work lives in meetings, though, I don't think I'm very controversial in saying there is a problem. Obviously, some meetings need to happen. But the notion that we need so many of them—with so many participants!—to successfully run our work lives is absolutely preposterous. Here are the critical ways to change the way you think about meetings, reduce the meetings you lead and attend, and make meetings more meaningful when you are there.

Use Email When You Can

The key to avoiding many unnecessary meetings is to do things in writing when you can. Especially these days, when seamless chat tools like Basecamp and Slack and Google Chat exist to make back-and-forth exchanges even more instantaneous than a regular email client, written communication is often infinitely faster in reaching certain goals than having a meeting. There is nothing more frustrating than multiple back-and-forth exchanges to schedule a meeting, then cancel a meeting, then reschedule a meeting, only to finally have it and find out the other person had a quick three-minute question! Although no one thinks they want more email, in terms of time efficiency, email often wins.

Use an Efficient Way to Schedule Meetings

If you do your own scheduling, you know that the

least efficient thing you can do is to email back and forth with someone about good times that you can connect. Instead, use a tool to help. If the others you're going to meet with are in your organization, encouraging everyone to keep their calendars updated makes this step irrelevant. If they aren't in your organization or you don't have access to their calendars, try a tool like Calendly.

Block Your Meetings

Remember to block schedule your meetings just as you block schedule other activities in your work life. If you are an introvert, like me, this also helps to deal with the fatigue that comes as the result of meetings.

Allow Buffer Time

This is especially critical if you schedule meetings using the block scheduling technique. Scheduling things back-to-back with no buffer is a recipe for chronic tardiness and stress. Instead, make sure to keep a small buffer between meetings to ensure you'll show up at the next one on time.

Schedule Meetings for the Amount of Time They Really Take

A great way to allow buffer time is also a great tip on

its own: don't schedule meetings for the preset thirty- and sixty-minute time slots that appear in your calendar system. People are much more likely to stay on the conference line for a full thirty minutes if it's been scheduled as such, even when they're done with the agenda after twenty. Instead, schedule meetings for the length of time you really need to get things done.

Be Clear if There Is an Agenda

As we have become more aware of some of the problems with meetings in corporate America, the idea that all meetings require an agenda has become a part of popular wisdom. In contrast, I do believe that some meetings simply do not have an agenda, and that's okay. Sometimes people just want to connect, which is important to maintain healthy relationships. In terms of time efficiency, though, it is important to schedule that catch-up, and not just have it spontaneously uproot your schedule and cause you to miss out on another activity you had blocked. Be up-front about its purpose, and you'll save your schedule.

Have an Agenda

The vast majority of meetings do require an agenda, and this is an important step in keeping things on track and on time. Work hard to create simple, clear agendas that everyone can follow. If other people need to prepare something, send the agenda ahead of time so that they can come with what is expected from them.

Be Careful of Standing Meetings

Oftentimes standing meetings (every week, or twice a week, say) are very necessary, and in my past I have regularly held standing meetings with bosses and with direct reports. The challenge is to make sure you aren't holding standing meetings on principle, and that you're doing it because it's truly needed. A great tip to reduce time spent on scheduling is to set up a weekly meeting with someone you think you might need to talk to two or three times a month, and then simply state that if it's not needed you will cancel a certain number of days (and not hours!) before.

Prepare When You Need to

If you are invited to a meeting and need to prepare, do so. This allows you to give your best effort to the other participants and sets the precedent for what you expect from others.

Only Go to Meetings Where You're Really Needed

If you work in a large organization, you likely have seen the number of meetings folks invite you to increase linearly with the number of years you've been at the company and the number of employees hired. Nip this in the bud and directly ask organizers to remove you from meetings that you aren't adding value to—or that fifteen other people can handle on their own.

Learn Positive Multitasking

The world is down on multitasking, and articles everywhere claim its demise: *Multitasking doesn't work. Mono-tasking is the new multitasking. Do more than one thing at a time and you're doing nothing at all.*

I agree that multitasking as we know it is broken. That said, I believe there is one type of multitasking that does reliably work.

As I've said before, I read a lot. And although this has always been true, it was the year that I discovered the power of positive multitasking that I really upped my reading goals. I did it through a little thing called audiobooks.

When I first read that combining "brainless" physical activities with mental activities is a great way to get more done, I realized that I was already doing this in my regular life, and that it was really a version of positive multitasking. I talked on the phone while cooking the tomato sauce I'd made a thousand times. I knitted while watching TV. And I listened to audiobooks while doing, well, anything.

When I first started talking about how listening to audiobooks had increased my reading goals on my blog, my friend Amalia responded in the comments:

When do you listen to these? I can't think of any time except exercise when I wouldn't just whip out a book/kindle instead? I'm intrigued.

Especially considering the fact that audiobooks often take longer than reading for most people (you likely read faster than you listen), this was a good question. After all, why bother to listen to an audiobook if you can read it faster, right? Wrong.

The benefit of an audiobook is that it enables positive multitasking, and not just when exercising. Here is when I find time to listen to audiobooks, and when you can do so (or do any other of your brain-"full" activities).

> *1. While Exercising*: I'm a huge fan of listening to an audiobook while running or working out. If you want to read and work out at the same time, you have to find a stationary bike (or subject your

treadmill to Kindle-induced nausea), but with an audiobook you can be doing anything.

2. *When in Transit*: Driving, taking public transport, or walking anywhere (through the grocery store, through an airport) are all easy times to listen to audiobooks when you wouldn't otherwise be able to read, and when most folks listen to music or nothing at all.

3. *While Eating*: Although you can read books while eating, it's never quite ideal. In contrast, listening to audiobooks is the perfect complement.

4. *While Doing Other Brainless Tasks*: Unloading the dishwasher? Cooking something you've made a thousand times? Putting on makeup? Nursing (sorry guys)? A perfect time to listen to an audiobook. Don't worry about putting on the headphones, just let your iPhone or other device play it on speaker. I do this all the time, and love the content I'm able to consume in an otherwise "down" moment.

As you might have guessed, many of the tips above don't only work with audiobooks. In fact, they work with all kinds of other brain-needy tasks as well. Inventor Nilofer Merchant is one of many innovators who has jumped on the bandwagon of walking meetings—taking meetings with coworkers while walking around the park, or up a mountain. This isn't a strategy that works only if your coworkers are up for the exercise, though. Having a walking meeting (or a walking call with a friend, family member, or friendly American Airlines representative) over the phone is a smart multitasking move, and has become even more common with the advent of treadmill desks. Bestselling author A. J. Jacobs is one of many people I know now using treadmill desks—and swearing by them.

Just be careful not to pant. During my long marathon training runs I was known for calling friends and family members to chat. One day, twenty minutes into a call, my friend Court asked, "Are you panting?" I confessed.

Remember the basics: positive multitasking combines a truly brainless activity with a brain-"full" activity. Or, said another way, a mental activity with a physical one.

S: STOP WORKING: KNOW WHEN AND HOW

FIND YOUR OASIS

In 2012, when I was working at Twitter, I went to both the Democratic and Republican national conventions. They were both crazy big events that involved nonstop meetings, long nights, and terrible fast food.

But then there was this thing called the Oasis.

The Oasis was the best thing that happened to me in those two weeks. It was Arianna Huffington's attempt to bring peace to the crazy, and boy did it work.

When I arrived in Tampa, I heard mention of this supposed hub of well-being and mindfulness. A place where anyone could go—free—and find peace and calm and books and food and—did I mention?—calm. As the whispers of other convention-goers became impossible to ignore, I knew I had to see it for myself. When I entered into the white-walled space from the Florida heat the first day, I already had high expectations.

Within five minutes, all such expectations were blown out of the water. It turns out that eating a lovely, healthy meal, perusing good books for your body and soul, and watching (and participating) in the yoga and meditation classes in session all around me were exactly the fuel I needed. The Oasis became *my* oasis at both conventions, and since that time, whenever I have found myself in a sterile conference space with thousands of other folks listening to the tenth speaker of the day, I long for such a special experience.

But the reality is that most busy events and busy days don't have an Oasis like the ones Huffington's team set up in Tampa or Charlotte that year. So it's important that we work to create them in the midst of our regular lives.

As Arianna Huffington says in *Thrive*, the point isn't to escape from it all and live on a Wyoming ranch—but rather to find a way to *live well* in the midst of our lives.

Here are some key ways to find your oasis to recharge during the day-to-day:

TAKE A MINI BREAK

One of the best ways to bring yourself back to the moment in a day of stress or overwhelm is just to pull your hands away from the keyboard, move your eyes to the window, and breathe. Let the thoughts come in, and let the thoughts flow out. And breathe all the while. I've heard it said that making sure your feet are on the floor at key moments of grounding can also help you feel more connected to what's going on around you. So try that as well as you breathe. And try the Time Out app on your computer to help remind you to do it.

FIND A MOMENT TO STOP

Mini breathing breaks are great, but what's even better is a ten- or fifteen-minute period of time where you can take a stop and do nothing, all for yourself. I find that the best way to do this—especially in a corporate environment where it's not necessarily possible to stare at the wall for fifteen minutes while others look on in wonder—is to take a short break to go on a walk. *Outside.*

They say that one of the best ways we can reduce stress is by getting out into the beautiful world around us. Indeed, nature is a great way to get the endorphins going and to kick your stress to the curb. Whether it's a beautiful park, a pristine botanical garden, or just a hotel balcony with a view, find nature and go there.

Combine it with a trip to get a coffee, say, or to run an errand you need to do. But in those ten minutes of walking, don't make phone calls. Don't listen to podcasts. Just walk and breathe and wait as the thoughts jamming your mind slowly rearrange themselves into calm.

It's all about finding those small moments where you take time out of the crazy, and finding time to disconnect from the speeding train of your life to bring your mind and heart back to calm.

TAP INTO POSITIVE EMOTIONS

You've likely heard it said that smiling makes you actually feel better. It's true, and I have more than one friend who swears by smiling in the mirror whenever she feels down. Positive emotions like hope are key to making sure your stress is as low as it can reasonably be. Every day, think of a way you can better tap into these key emotions and cultivate the side of your heart and mind that wants to feel happiness. A great way to do this in the midst of your life is to find something you love to do and weave it into your workday.

One of my friends has a demanding job as a physical therapist. Given her long days, she used to find it incredibly helpful to take a minute out of her day to rejuvenate—and she got creative to do so. At lunchtime she'd look for an open room where she could read a novel for thirty minutes by herself as she ate her lunch. It cleared her head and recharged her for the afternoon. Even if you're not an obsessive reader like I am, it turns out that the act of sitting down, resting, and reading a good novel can really make you feel better. The key is to immerse yourself in a story—and not a nonfiction business book—to really turn your mood around.

QUIT SOMETHING TODAY

"Every single Thursday, I quit something."—Bob Goff

Another way to limit your activities to your best work is to make a consistent, regular routine of taking things off your plate.

My friend Bob Goff is famous for doing just this, and for encouraging others to do the same. Bob has a crazy full life: he runs a law firm and a nonprofit organization, serves as the honorary consul to the Republic of Uganda, is a bestselling author, and has a vibrant community of friends and family he takes pride in spending regular time with. Every day, Bob pops up in my email or my Instagram feed doing amazing things somewhere in the world: helping kids in northern Iraq, building a chapel on a remote British Columbian island, and cheering on his friends wherever they are. In order to accomplish all this, he has to make sure he's not doing what he shouldn't.

This is true of all of us. Every day, we continue to do things—or take on new things—that don't connect with our true passions or goals. Little by little, we stuff our lives and lose our way in the process. Bob attacked this problem directly by starting to quit one single thing every Thursday. As he learned, the single act of cutting down and cutting back can have an incredible cascading effect in your life. Even if it's not Thursday, choose one thing you can quit today. Try it again next week. Slowly but surely you'll work to pare down your life.

TAKE A WEEKEND OFF

Two days isn't a lot of time. And, as many of us know, two days can easily be taken up with shuttling kids back and forth to sports practices and birthday parties. To make our weekends count, we have to find a real break from work, and a real way to rejuvenate for the week ahead.

Laura Vanderkam, author of *What the Most Successful People Do on the Weekend*, suggests a great strategy for making sure you are maximizing rejuvenation in your weekends, and it's all about something she calls "anchor events." The concept is this: Choose a few pleasurable activities you want to do over your weekend, and schedule them in. It may be "bake a cake with my daughter on Saturday," or "watch a movie as a family on Friday night," or "go biking with a friend."

Whatever your anchor events are, by scheduling in this fun time, you'll be able to take advantage of the happiness we all get from the anticipation of them. Additionally, you'll come to the end of your weekend feeling like you truly enjoyed yourself and didn't fritter the time away with reality TV marathons. In general, the strategy of scheduling downtime doesn't require a whole weekend, and can also work well even in an afternoon.

TAKE A VACATION

With a longer period of time on the table, the stakes are higher, and the potential for rest and rejuvenation is even greater.

They say that 57 percent of Americans don't take all their vacation days each year, and I'm surely not the only one who thinks there's a problem with that.[10] A vacation is the perfect pause that more of us need in our work lives. A good time-out can reenergize and refocus you to win, and vacations are great opportunities to do just this.

Marisa Mayer, CEO of Yahoo, is known for taking a one-week vacation every four months.[11] For her, the reward for four months of head-down work is getting one week off to play. Critically, though, time off is not just about playing. As Mayer says, it's really about recharging. We need time off to make our time "on" really count.

Author Michael Hyatt, who used to work in corporate America as the CEO of Thomas Nelson, now works for himself, allowing him to take a sabbatical each summer. He values this time immensely. Ken Blanchard, the San Diego–based business author who has sold over twenty-one million copies of his many books, spends his summers at his lake house in New York. Although he does do some work, he prioritizes relaxing time with friends and family.

Although we often hear about the importance of starting things, we easily forget that starting only works if we take regular stops as well. And as these leaders show, stops can come in all shapes and sizes. A digital one, I believe, can prove one of the best kinds.

DIGITALLY DISCONNECT

When I started tracking the time I spent online, one of my clear goals was to reduce that time. I wanted to be more productive, with less wasted time spent staring at a flat screen. I've often found that if I'm not being productive in the middle of my day and find myself on my dreaded Internet loop (email, Twitter, Instagram, CNN, email, Twitter, Instagram, repeat), stepping away from my computer is the single best thing I can do to refocus my priorities.

On the weekends, I take the same approach. By keeping my computer off for at least one full day—and hopefully two—I can "detox" enough so that, come Monday morning, I'm excited to dive back in. Stepping away also makes the heart grow fonder, of course.

A few years ago, I started to explore the idea of taking longer digital breaks or "digital detoxes," and along the way I learned a number of key lessons about how important getting away from our screens is, and how to create truly effective digital detoxes.

Here are some key things to remember when considering a digital break:

Decide What Kind of Break It Will Be

The first key step in any break-taking is figuring out what exactly you're taking a break from. A break from social media? A break from email? A break from the Internet at large? A break from all flat screens? There are a variety of different types of digital breaks. In *The Winter of Our Disconnect*, Susan Maushart eschewed all flat screens from the house for six months—but allowed herself to use her computer outside of the home to meet her writing deadlines. Baratunde Thurston left the Internet for twenty-five days—and turned off text messages. Author Kyle Tennant in *Unfriend Yourself: Three days to Detox, Discern, and Decide about Social Media* promotes the idea of taking a fast from social media in particular. One person I read about allowed one email check per day. Different breaks can work for different aims.

The key is to define what the break is in specific terms. Then go a step further and write it down so you won't be confused. When I took a twelve-day digital detox, I did just that, filling my journal with constant reminders of what I was doing a la *"You are on a complete digital detox, Claire. Remember!"*

Set Your Break Boundaries and Stick to Them

Boundaries are always tough, and your break boundaries are just as challenging. Even on a social media break, say, you might wake up one morning with an insatiable itch to scroll through Facebook for the teams of babies born in your network overnight. Don't do it. A break is a break, and if you've decided to take one, uphold your boundaries.

A total tech blackout is sometimes a good thing, as I learned on my twelve-day complete digital break. The first couple of mornings I could practically feel the shakes as I tried to reach for my iPhone to scroll my emails and tweets before getting out of bed. My only "cheat" was to receive text messages if something crazy happened and I had to get online. Another year on vacation, I decided I wasn't into such a total blackout, so instead I did a very scaled-back version of a detox, staying off my computer but checking emails occasionally on my iPhone. Since I rarely respond to many emails on my iPhone, it kept me out of the email fray.

Prepare Beforehand

Depending on the level of intensity of your digital detox, you've got to plan. Write blog posts, schedule social media updates, and set auto-responders on your email addresses alerting folks. Especially if you are going offline for more than a few days, making sure that you've got a good auto-response is key. Importantly, you've got to do it right in order to encourage folks to not expect a response, and not try to contact you through other means. On my twelve-day total digital detox, I encouraged folks in my auto-responder to "text me if needed." The result? A number of non-urgent texts coming. Next time, I know to use *much* stronger language.

Alert the Important Folks

There are folks who just might need to know when you're stepping out of life for a little while. Friends and family who might wonder why you're not responding at once to every long cat pic they send? A client you're working with on a project due after your break will end? An assistant who will need to help out just a bit more while you're away? All these people need to be in the loop—and doing so beforehand (and then reiterating with an out-of-office response message that conveys clear information on when you'll be back and how to deal with things while you're gone) is essential.

Make It Public

Another benefit to telling your friends and family what you're doing: it will encourage them to keep you on track. Tell them to slap your wrist, or guide you gently toward the ink and quill for your communication needs.

Start Your Day Right

As you might imagine, a perfect offline morning shouldn't start with you tweeting from the pillow. Instead, use your digital detox to tap into your offline morning routine. When consciously trying to disconnect, what you do first thing in the morning is more important than ever.

Have a Backup Plan

There is always the chance that someone really needs to get in touch, and so it's a good idea to have a backup plan. Whether that means hiring someone to help out (or tasking a current hire with the job), or checking texts on occasion for urgent messages, think of the way that you'll feel both digitally disconnected and responsible at the same time.

Working better is about stopping more, and don't let anyone tell you differently. Stop the madness, get the break you need, and watch your productivity soar.

CONCLUSION

In this book we've explored what it means to live in a world where there are too many things on our plate. This is our reality, and it's not going away. As such, my goal is to enjoy more of life in the midst of the busy journey. The way to do this, I believe, lies in understanding how to do better work. The teachings in this book are the exact strategies I have used in my own life to do as much as I do—and to (usually) not feel harried in the process. It is a process, and one I work at every day. The Do Less method, for me, has been nothing short of transformative. I believe it can work nicely in your own world as well. The key is to take the time, do the work, and then reap the rewards. Ultimately, it's about doing your best work, and finding more time for living along the way.

That said, none of this living is worth it if you don't have a clear idea of what you're living for. Each of us has an inner compass telling us why we're here and what we want out of this time on earth—to pursue the calling of our life, to raise our family well, to be a leader in our faith or community, to serve as a source of motivation for the world. For me, that means discovering why God put me on earth at this particular time and place and then doing that thing He wants me to do. Finding clarity on what your vision is for a life of happiness and fulfillment is absolutely essential. Living well means nothing if you don't have the meaning behind your life to hold up to the light. Your meaning might differ from that of your neighbor's, but what won't differ is its existence. We all have something that drives us and that makes the journey worth every step. The key is to figure out what it is so you can determine how you want to live. Then do everything you can to make as much time for that living.

RECOMMENDED FOR FURTHER READING

Here are some of my favorite books on productivity, goal setting, mindfulness, and balancing it all.

- *The Balance Within*, Esther M. Sternberg
- *Eat that Frog: 21 Ways to Stop Procrastinating and Get More Done in Less Time*, Brian Tracy
- *New Slow City*, William Powers
- *The Four-Hour Work Week*, Tim Ferriss
- *The One Minute Manager*, Ken Blanchard
- *Rework*, Jason Fried and David Heinemeier Hansson
- *What the Most Successful People Do Before Breakfast*, Laura Vanderkam
- *The Power of Full Engagement*, Jim Loehr and Tony Schwartz
- *The Power of Habit*, Charles Duhigg

- *Flow: The Psychology of Optimal Experience,* Mihály Csíkszentmihályi
- *The Willpower Instinct,* Kelly McGonigal
- *The Winter of Our Disconnect,* Susan Maushart
- *The Best Yes,* Lysa Terkeurst
- *The Fringe Hours,* Jessica Turner
- *The Way We're Working Isn't Working,* Tony Schwartz
- *The Clockwork Muse,* Eviatar Zerubavel
- *Bird by Bird,* Anne Lamott
- *Accidental Genius, Using Writing to Generate Your Best Ideas, Insight, and Content,* Mark Levy
- *Start: Punch Fear in the Face, Escape Average, and Do Work That Matters,* Jon Acuff
- *Vision Map: Charting a Step-by-Step Course for Your Biggest Hopes and Dreams,* Joël Malm
- *The Well-Balanced World Changer,* Sarah Cunningham
- *The Happiness Project,* Gretchen Rubin
- *Internal Time,* Till Roenneberg
- *Unfriend Yourself: Three days to Detox, Discern, and Decide about Social Media,* Kyle Tennant
- *The Better Life: Small Things You Can Do Right Where You Are,* Claire Diaz-Ortiz

NOTES

1. Mark Levy, *Accidental Genius: Using Writing to Generate Your Best Ideas, Insight, and Content* (San Francisco: Berrett-Koehler Publishers, 2010).

2. Paul J. Meyer, *Attitude Is Everything: If You Want to Succeed Above and Beyond* (Meyer Resource Group, 2003).

3. http://www.nydailynews.com/life-style/average-american-watches-5-hours-tv-day-article-1.1711954.

4. http://www.theguardian.com/housing-network/2012/dec/17/ban-staff-email-halton-housing-trust.

5. http://mashable.com/2012/04/05/sheryl-sandberg-leaves-work-at-530/.

6. http://gorowe.com/.

7. https://www.psychologytoday.com/blog/brain-wise/201209/the-true-cost-multi-tasking.

8. http://www.huffingtonpost.com/2012/08/01/email-work-day_n_1725728.html; http://www.theguardian.com/housing-network/2012/dec/17/ban-staff-email-halton-housing-trust.

9. https://www.themuse.com/advice/how-much-time-do-we-spend-in-meetings-hint-its-scary.

10. http://www.cnn.com/2011/TRAVEL/05/23/vacation.in.america/index.html.

11. http://www.businessinsider.com/successful-people-who-barely-sleep-2012-9.

ABOUT
THE AUTHOR

Claire Diaz-Ortiz is an author, speaker, and technology innovator who has been named one of the 100 Most Creative People in Business by *Fast Company*. Claire was an early employee at Twitter, Inc., where she led social innovation.

In Claire's time at Twitter, she was called everything from "The Woman Who Got the Pope on Twitter" (*Wired*) and "Twitter's Pontiff Recruitment Chief" (*The Washington Post*) to a "Force for Good" (*Forbes*) and "One of the Most Generous People in Social Media" (*Fast Company*).

Claire is the author of several books, including, *Twitter for Good: Change the World One Tweet at a Time; Greater Expectations: Succeed (and Stay Sane) in an On-Demand, All-Access, Always-On Age; Hope Runs: An American Tourist, a Kenyan Boy, a Journey of Redemption;* and *The Better Life: Small Things You Can Do Right Where You Are.*

She is a frequent international speaker on social media, business, and innovation and has been invited to deliver keynotes and trainings at organizations like the Vatican, the US State Department, Verizon, South by Southwest, TEDX, and many others.

She writes a popular business blog at ClaireDiaz Ortiz.com and serves as a LinkedIn Influencer, one of a select group of several hundred global leaders chosen to provide original content on the LinkedIn platform.

Claire holds an MBA from Oxford University, where she was a Skoll Foundation Scholar for Social Entrepreneurship, and has a BA and an MA in anthropology from Stanford University.

She is the cofounder of Hope Runs, a nonprofit organization operating in AIDS orphanages in Kenya.

She has appeared widely in television and print news sources such as CNN, BBC, *Time*, *Newsweek*, *The New York Times*, *Good Morning America*, *The Today Show*, *The Washington Post*, *Fortune*, *Forbes*, *Fast Company*, and many others.

Read more about her at
www.ClaireDiazOrtiz.com or via @claire on Twitter.

PERSONAL REFLECTION

moody
collective

Join our email newsletter list to get resources and
encouragement as you build a deeper faith.

Moody Collective brings words of life to a generation seeking deeper faith. We are a part of Moody Publishers, representing this next generation of followers of Christ through books on creativity, travel, the gospel, storytelling, decision making, leadership, and more.

We seek to know, love, and serve the millennial generation with grace and humility. Each of our books is intended to challenge and encourage our readers as they pursue God.

When you sign up for our newsletter, you'll get our emails twice a month. These will include the best of the resources we've seen online, book deals and giveaways, plus behind-the-scenes and extra content from our books and authors. Sign up at *www.moodycollective.com.*

a part of Moody Publishers

More from
Claire Diaz-Ortiz

Vision Map is a template to start anyone on the path to envisioning and experiencing a God-given dream. God often gives us a difficult problem to solve, and we just need a push in the right direction to find the answer.

Where are you heading?

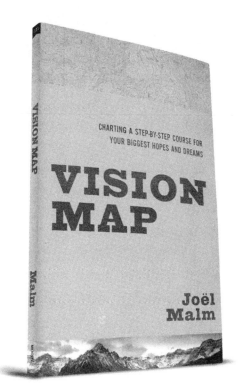

MOODY
Publishers™

From the Word to Life

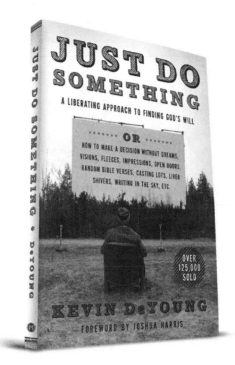

God doesn't need to tell us what to do at each fork in the road. He already revealed His plan for our lives: love Him with our whole hearts, obey His Word, and after that, do what we like. No reason to be directionally challenged. **Just do something.**

MOODY
Publishers™

From the Word to Life

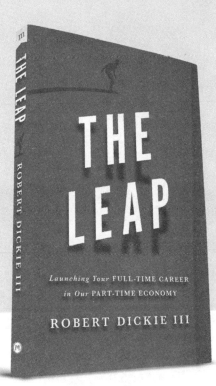

THE LEAP

Launching Your FULL-TIME CAREER
in Our PART-TIME ECONOMY

ROBERT DICKIE III

College graduates are facing large student loans and high unemployment rates. Older generations are feeling the effects of the recession as they lose stable jobs and are forced to find new work. The old economy is fading away and a new economy is rising in its place. To succeed in the new economy, we must take a mental leap, rethinking our strategies for success.

moody
collective

MOODY
Publishers™

MOODYCOLLECTIVE.COM